D1089004

Creative Writing
in 5 Simple Steps

Write a
Mystery
in 5 Simple Steps

Amy Dunkleberger

Enslow Publishers, Inc.
40 Industrial Road
Box 398
Berkeley Heights, NJ 07922
USA
http://www.enslow.com

Library of Congress Cataloging-in-Publication Data

Dunkleberger, Amy.
  Write a mystery in 5 simple steps / Amy Dunkleberger.
      p. cm. — (Creative writing in 5 simple steps)
  Summary: "Divides the creative writing process into five steps, from inspiration to publishable story, and includes in-depth treatment of the mystery fiction genre with writing prompts"—Provided by publisher.
  Includes bibliographical references and index.
  ISBN 978-0-7660-3835-6
  1. Detective and mystery stories—Authorship—Juvenile literature. I. Title.
  PN3377.5.D4D86 2012
  808.3'872—dc22

                            2010037618

Future editions:
Paperback ISBN 978-1-4644-0097-1
ePUB ISBN 978-1-4645-1004-5
PDF ISBN 978-1-4646-1004-2

Printed in the United States of America

032012 Lake Book Manufacturing, Inc., Melrose Park, IL

10 9 8 7 6 5 4 3 2 1

To Our Readers: We have done our best to make sure all Internet Addresses in this book were active and appropriate when we went to press. However, the author and the publisher have no control over and assume no liability for the material available on those Internet sites or on other Web sites they may link to. Any comments or suggestions can be sent by e-mail to comments@enslow.com or to the address on the back cover.

Every effort has been made to locate all copyright holders of material used in this book. If any errors or omissions have occurred, corrections will be made in future editions of this book.

♲ Enslow Publishers, Inc., is committed to printing our books on recycled paper. The paper in every book contains 10% to 30% post-consumer waste (PCW). The cover board on the outside of each book contains 100% PCW. Our goal is to do our part to help young people and the environment too!

Cover and Illustration Credits: Shutterstock.com.

Contents

Book Key

Keeping a Journal

On the Web

Genre History

Fun Fact

Check It Out!

Writer's Block

Here's an Idea!

Your Assignment

Organizer

Daydreaming

Step 1

Finding Your Mystery Muse

Was it Professor Plum in the kitchen with the candlestick? Or Colonel Mustard in the conservatory with the wrench? Chances are, you know these colorful characters from the *Clue* mystery game. Chances are, *Clue* is only one of many mysteries you have already experienced in your life.

Books, movies, TV shows, video games . . . mysteries can be found everywhere, for every type of audience. Part story, part puzzle, mysteries are naturally fun and exciting, both to read and to write.

But how do you begin to write a mystery story? Perhaps you have heard the adage "write what you know" and wondered how you could "know" enough to invent a believable mystery.

Your Muse

Mysteries can be full-length novels (usually more than 140 pages), short stories (usually less than 30 pages), and any length in between. Regardless of length, all stories begin with an original idea, a spark that starts the creative fire. The idea might come in the form of a character or an event. In the case of mysteries, the character will likely be a detective of some sort—the person who solves the mystery—and the event will be a crime.

But where do you find inspiration for these original ideas? Your muse, or source of inspiration, can come from many places. Music, paintings, news articles, dreams, and your own life experiences can spur ideas. Inspiration can come in an apparent flash, as it did for author Jacqueline Winspear, creator of the Maisie Dobbs mystery series: "I was inspired to write my first novel, *Maisie Dobbs,* by the character herself, who appeared in my mind's eye as I allowed my imagination to wander while stuck in traffic. . . . By the time I started my car to drive home, I had the entire story in my head."[1]

 ## Ideas for Ideas

When coming up with ideas for stories, many writers look to their own lives for inspiration. Caroline Lawrence used her background in archaeology as the jumping-off point for her Roman Mysteries series. Newspaper reporter John Feinstein mined his knowledge of sports to come up with his sports-themed mystery series. Experiences in a specific activity, such as sports and special-interest clubs, can be an excellent source for story ideas. They can also provide a good arena around which to build a tight story.

Some authors have developed special techniques for zeroing in on story ideas. In an online interview, children's writer Nancy Springer, for example, revealed that she finds inspiration by talking with strangers: "I will start strange conversations just to see what people will say. Almost always, they'll come up with something that I never would have thought of."[2]

R. L. Stine, author of the Goosebumps, Nightmare Room, and Fear Street series, refers to his sources of inspiration as his "idea store." Stine divides his store into three "departments"—the experience department, the memory department, and the "what if" or "wonder" department.

For experience ideas, Stine starts with everyday activities—a bus ride or a trip to the movies, for example—and finds ways to twist these ordinary actions into a compelling story. Observation is a key element of experience ideas. The more the writer notices, the more material he or she will have for forming fresh ideas.

Stine's memory ideas come from recollections of people and art that have lingered in his imagination. A lyric in a song or a past conversation with a friend might provide the perfect jumping-off point for a story. Being "true" to the memory is not important. Once it has inspired you, you can change it to suit your creative needs.

Stine's "what if" or "wonder" ideas begin with a question: "What would happen if . . . ?" The opening line of Stine's Fear Street mystery *The Confession* is a perfect example of a "what if" idea: "What would you do if one of your best friends took you aside and confessed to you he had *killed* someone?"[3]

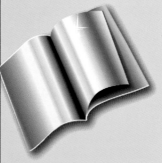

A Little Mystery History

Mystery stories have been around for a long time. Some historians trace the origins of the mystery genre all the way back to ancient Greece and Rome. Modern mysteries emerged in the 1800s, after such cities as Paris, New York, and London had formed large-scale police forces.

American author Edgar Allan Poe (1809–1849) is considered the father of modern mystery writing. His 1841 short story "The Murders in the Rue Morgue" introduced readers to Auguste C. Dupin, fiction's first crime-solving detective. Other early mystery writers include English author Wilkie Collins (1824–1889) and American writers Louisa May Alcott (1832–1888) and Anna Katharine Green (1846–1935). Ebenezer Gryce, the hero of Green's 1878 novel *The Leavenworth Case*, was the first fictional detective created by a female writer.

Beginning in the late 1800s, Sir Arthur Conan Doyle (1859–1930) took mystery fiction to the next level with his still-popular Sherlock Holmes series. Doyle crafted great stories, but his main achievement was the creation of Holmes, his brilliant and resourceful private detective.

The early twentieth century marked the next great wave of mystery fiction. Agatha Christie (1890–1976), the "queen of crime," wrote the first of her eighty-plus novels in 1920.

Christie was soon joined by fellow English author Dorothy L. Sayers (1893–1957) and American writer S. S. Van Dyne (1888–1939), among many others. Around the same time, the Nancy Drew and Hardy Boys series became the first mysteries written expressly for teens.

Like Doyle, Christie and Sayers specialized in cozy mysteries. In cozies, the crime has already been committed when the story begins, and the story contains little or no violence. Often the crimes occur in isolated locations, such as a cruise ship or a mansion. Cozies are almost always whodunits—stories in which the identity of the criminal is unknown until the end.

Also in the twentieth century, two other types of mystery emerged: the police procedural and the hard-boiled detective story. Unlike cozies, police procedurals and hard-boiled detective stories often depict violent crimes and feature sleuths who are tough and fearless. Crimes in police procedurals are solved by policemen, while hard-boiled detectives are typically "private eyes" who work outside the police department. Sometimes the criminal in these mysteries is known to the reader from the start.

Americans Dashiell Hammett (1894–1961) and Raymond Chandler (1888–1959) pioneered the hard-boiled detective story, and Ed McBain (1926–2005) was one of the first authors to master and to popularize the police procedural.

Check Out These Mystery Series

To become a good mystery writer, you should read as many well-written mysteries as you can. The book series listed below represent both long-standing favorites and newer entries into the world of kids' mysteries. Check them out at your local library or bookstore.

The Enola Holmes Mysteries by Nancy Springer
In this series, tomboy sleuth Enola Holmes, the younger sister of master detective Sherlock Holmes, uses her intelligence and spunk to solve crimes and unmask criminals.

Fear Street by R. L. Stine
The students of Shadyside High provide the eerie crimes as well as the tough solutions in Stine's popular Fear Street series.

The Houdini and Nate Mystery Series by Tom Lalicki
Set in New York in the early 1900s, these mysteries pair real-life escape artist Harry Houdini with fictional twelve-year-old Nate.

The Hardy Boys by Franklin W. Dixon
First published in 1927, these books were written by different ghostwriters under the pseudonym Franklin W. Dixon. Follow teenage brothers Frank and Joe Hardy as they solve crimes in their small town of Bayport, throughout the United States, and all over the world.

Nancy Drew by Carolyn Keene
Written by various authors under the pen name Carolyn Keene, these mysteries, around since 1929, feature the original "girl sleuth." The series has expanded to include graphic novels and challenging video games.

The Roman Mysteries by Caroline Lawrence
In Lawrence's carefully researched mystery series, a diverse team of four young detectives follow clues and track down criminals in ancient Rome.

Sammy Keyes by Wendelin Van Draanen
While struggling with her fractured family life, spunky sleuth Sammy Keyes investigates all manners of crime in her small California town.

Last Shot series by John Feinstein
Teen journalists Stevie Thomas and Susan Carol Anderson use their news-gathering skills to interrogate suspects and solve crimes in the world of sports.

Theodore Boone by John Grisham
Best-selling author John Grisham's children's mystery series chronicles the exploits of thirteen-year-old would-be lawyer Theodore Boone.

As the story unfolds, Stine answers all the questions he poses. But knowing all the answers to what-if questions in advance is not crucial to devising a solid story idea.

You may not always be aware of the creative process going on in your head, but you will recognize the results when they happen. According to Springer, "Ideas usually come just a little bit at a time . . . a whiff in the air, something that zips past. You have to grab it. Sometimes, it's just a feeling, an emotion, a picture in your head."[4]

 ## Keep a Journal

Journals have long been a favorite tool of writers and are an excellent way to generate story ideas. You can write in them as you would a diary or use them simply to record ideas as they pop into your head. Be sure to make note of things that stimulate your senses—wet dogs, loud music, rainbows, etc. Include funny comments and other scraps of conversation you hear during the day. Record your reactions to movies and TV shows—anything that makes you think and feel!

Whether you are adding a single sentence or a whole page, you should try to write in your journal every day. A journal can be a formal bound book, with blank pages, or an inexpensive spiral notebook. Small is best, so you can carry it with you and be ready to jot down new ideas as they come.

You may also want to record your thoughts on video or tape. But learning to express yourself in writing, even informally, will help sharpen your literary skills and make story writing easier down the line.

Writing Exercises

Published authors find inspiration for their stories in many ways. To discover your mystery muse, try one or both of the following activities:

1. Take an ordinary event from your life—a birthday party, a family vacation, the first day of school, a sporting event, etc.—and think of ways it could be turned into a mystery. For instance, what if the birthday presents at the party disappeared? What if the girl in the motel room next door suddenly changed appearances? What if the fire alarm went off at school? What if the star athlete went missing halfway through the game?

2. In a local newspaper or online news source, find a report about a crime committed in your area. In your journal, list all the facts of the crime that are mentioned in the article—the who, what, where, when, and how. Imagine you are the detective investigating the case. Which details of the crime stand out to you? Who would you talk to first?

Step 2

Plotting the Puzzle

A mystery is a bit like a jigsaw puzzle whose pieces have been spread across a table. Each piece contains information about a crime, and when all the pieces are put together correctly, the story of the crime is revealed. Your job as a mystery writer is to create the puzzle pieces, then lay them all out so the reader can connect them in proper order. The task is challenging, but you can begin by identifying the pieces you will need to build a good mystery puzzle.

The Crime

Every mystery puzzle needs at least one crime, but the crime does not have to be violent or complicated. It does need to be believable, however. The reader has to believe that your villain is physically and mentally capable of committing the deed. Crimes that appear frequently in mysteries written for and by teens include theft, blackmail, vandalism, missing persons, and fraud.

For maximum impact, the crime to be solved should be revealed at the beginning of the story. The rest of the story's action (its plot) flows out of this opening crime.

In *Nancy Drew: The Case of the Lost Song*, the theft of an old tape recording sets the mystery in motion. The main crime in the Enola Holmes's mystery *The Case of the Bizarre Bouquets* is the kidnapping of Dr. Watson, Sherlock Holmes's partner.

Mystery short stories (under thirty pages) need only one crime to be effective. In longer mysteries, secondary crimes are often included to add twists and keep the reader engaged. In *The Case of the Lost Song*, as Nancy works to uncover the thief's identity, for instance, more antiques are stolen, and Nancy is attacked by an unseen assailant. These secondary crimes, however, relate to the original crime and are not separate mysteries to be solved.

The Solution

Mysteries must have a solution. By the end of the story, the reader must know who committed the crime and why. Often authors will figure out the solution first and work backward from the end of the story. Knowing how your story ends before you start writing will help you stay on the right path.

The Clues

A clue, or lead, is any piece of information that helps the detective identify suspects and reveal the mystery's solution. Clues can be discovered through interrogation— the questioning of witnesses or suspects by the detective.

Mysteries on the Web

Playing mystery games is a fun and effective way to learn about the parts that make up the genre. The Web site MysteryNet contains many interactive mystery stories and puzzles, including Solve-it, See-n-Solve, and Get-a-Clue.

Solve-it invites the reader to identify the criminal from among a group of suspects. See-n-Solve asks the reader to investigate a crime scene by clicking different items that reveal clues. Get-a-Clue challenges the reader to see how many clues it takes for the reader to solve the mystery. These games can give you a better understanding of how your audience will work through your own story to solve the crime.

They can also be found through investigation, such as looking up an old news story on the Internet or searching a suspect's belongings.

Clues should appear throughout your story in logical fashion. Each one should contain enough information to be useful, but not so much as to give away the solution too soon.

A red herring, on the other hand, is information that misleads and distracts the detective. Red herrings, or false leads, appear at first to be real clues. Often they are invented by the criminal to cast suspicion on another person. Sometimes, however, the detective's suspicions are just wrong. For instance, in *Sisters of Mercy*, Sammy Keyes follows a teen runaway she suspects of some church thefts but eventually learns that the runaway is not involved in the crime. Include both clues and red herrings in your story.

Evidence and Deduction

By themselves, clues are meaningless. When strung together by the detective, however, clues become evidence, or proof, of a suspect's guilt. Looking at the evidence and coming to a conclusion about its meaning is called deduction. Detectives make deductions about who committed the crime based on the evidence they have gathered.

The Suspects

All mysteries need suspects. A suspect is any character who appears to have a motive, or reason, for committing the crime. Often suspects are eliminated through alibis. Alibis establish the suspects' innocence by showing they were in another location when the crime was committed. Alibis can be checked out by the detective and confirmed as true or false.

Witnesses are any characters who saw the crime, or any activity, such as a getaway, directly related to the crime. Many clues come from statements made by witnesses. Not all crimes have witnesses, however. Some witnesses may also be suspects.

Building Suspense

Taken by itself, a good puzzle is fun, but it is not dramatic. Mysteries become exciting when the writer builds suspense. One way to build suspense, or dramatic tension, is through action. Some activities, such as chases, escapes, and fights, are naturally suspenseful.

Suspense can also be created through pacing. As you near the end of your story, the pace, or tempo, of the action should get faster and faster, like a sprint at the end of a race. By then, the reader should know who all the characters are as well as their motives and alibis.

Once the detective has put the puzzle pieces together and deduced the crime's solution, he or she should move quickly to reveal the criminal's identity. At the same time, the detective should confront and publicly expose the criminal in some way. Confrontations usually end with the guilty party being arrested by the authorities.

Keeping Track of Your Puzzle Pieces

Because mystery plots are very structured, keeping track of the who, what, where, when, and how is vital. There are many ways to organize story elements, including step sheets, charts, and/or index cards. Similar to an outline, a step sheet is a numbered step-by-step list of the story's main plot points, from beginning to end. Each step, or plot point, is described in a sentence or two and leads logically to the next step.

To keep track of suspects, clues, deductions, and solutions, you can create a chart by answering the questions below:

Story Elements Organizer

✔ What is the crime? Who committed it? Who solves it? Who are the suspects?

✔ Where is the story set? Where does the crime take place?

✔ What are the clues? (List them in order.) How are they revealed? Who finds them?

✔ What are the red herrings? What are the obstacles?

✔ What are the deductions? (List them in order.)

✔ What is the solution? How is it revealed?

Index Cards

If you are writing a longer mystery, you may want to organize your story by breaking it down on index cards, scene by scene. Every time your story moves to a new location, you have a new scene. Each scene should have its own index card. Each card should include the following information:

1. The location or setting of the scene.

2. The characters who appear in the scene.

3. The action of the scene. What happens?

4. What clues or red herrings are revealed in the scene?

5. What is the purpose of the scene? (Introduce a suspect, eliminate a suspect, make a deduction, etc.)

Clear the Clutter!

If you are having trouble getting started on your story, you may need to "power down." Clearing your mind of mental clutter can help get your creative juices flowing. To remove clutter, shut off all your electronic devices and games and find a quiet place to relax. (You can even lie down.) Close your eyes and try to make your mind as blank as possible. Begin to ask yourself questions about your story: Who is my detective? What is the crime? Where is it set? Allow your imagination to take over, or as Jacqueline Winspear described it, allow your imagination "to wander."

To get a sense of your story's flow, pin the completed cards on a board or spread them out on a flat surface. Does the order, or timeline, of the scenes make sense? Does one scene lead naturally into the next? Does each scene have a clear purpose? Does each scene offer new information, or is it repetitive? One advantage of the index card method is how easy it is to add, remove, or rearrange scenes if your original timeline doesn't work.

You might find it helpful to use all the aforementioned organizing methods. There is no right way to keep track of your story elements. Everyone processes things differently. Choose whatever methods work best for you.

Writing Exercises

1. Create a story elements organizer similar to the one earlier in this chapter. You can draw one using a ruler, or devise one on a computer. Fill in the sections based on your Step 1 incident or situation.

2. Using the incident or situation you invented for Step 1, break your story into scenes beginning with the last scene. Working backward from the crime's solution, list the main elements of each scene on index cards.

Step 3

Daring Detectives, Clever Criminals—Creating 3-D Characters

In the *Mystery Writer's Handbook*, editor Lawrence Treat details the rules of the classic mystery. His first rule is very simple: the mystery must contain at least one crime or misdeed, and the reader must want to see the crime solved. The first half of Treat's rule flows from the story's plot. The second half of the rule—wanting to see the crime solved—is achieved primarily through the story's characters. Figuring out the identities of your main characters is one of the first decisions you will make as a mystery writer.

The Hero of Our Story Is . . .

In mystery stories, the protagonist, or hero, is either a professional detective—a policeman or private investigator—or an amateur detective. Any type of person can be an amateur detective, as long as he or she is capable of solving the crime. In mysteries written for teens, the detective is always an amateur, although a real detective might appear in the story as a helper.

Some amateur detectives, such as Nancy Drew, act almost like real detectives. They are known for their sleuthing skills and are sometimes asked to solve difficult cases. Enola Holmes, Sherlock Holmes's fictional sister, is a secret amateur detective. Others, such as Sammy Keyes and the Roman Mysteries foursome, are reluctant detectives. They stumble on crimes and become involved almost by accident.

Whether deliberate or reluctant, your detective should be appealing and believable so your readers will want to solve the mystery with you.

What are qualities that make mystery detectives appealing and believable?

✔ First and foremost they must care about other people and have a sense of right and wrong. They must be champions of justice. They must strive to make things right, sometimes risking their own safety to do so.

 # Biographies

Many writers create mini-biographies of their characters before starting their stories. Biographies help authors keep track of their "players" and can inspire them to create multi-layered personas. Biographies typically include facts and background information about each character. They provide practical information, such as age and occupation, and details about the characters' personalities and skills.

✔ Second, your detective must be clever. In order to follow clues, your sleuth must be able to see connections between people and actions. "Book smarts" are not always required (though they can help), but sharp, clear thinking is.

✔ Third, your detective must be hard working and active. Lazy sleuths are boring. Your detective should initiate action, not wait for things to happen.

✔ Last, to make your hero believable and likable, he or she should have flaws. Knowing right from wrong does not mean the character is perfect—far from it. The most interesting detectives have flaws and make mistakes. They stumble. Sammy Keyes, for example, is loud and impulsive and often ends up in trouble for acting out. The teen heroes of the Fear Street stories will lie to avoid punishment and to impress their friends. Faults like these make detectives more realistic and recognizable to the reader.

Suspects and Villains

Treat's second rule of mystery writing is that the criminal, like the detective, must appear early and often in the story. After the detective, the criminal, the villain, is the most important character in a mystery. However, depending on the type of mystery you are telling, the reader may not know which character is the villain until the very end of the story.

In whodunits, the villain is hidden among a group of suspects. Writers usually make suspects as different from one another as possible—different ages, races, occupations, etc. Some suspects may have questionable traits or backgrounds—a gang member with a police record, for instance, or a teacher with a bad temper.

In other mysteries, the villain is identified early on, and the story's action involves stopping the criminal activity. In John Feinstein's *Last Shot: A Final Four Mystery*, for example, the student detectives overhear the bad guy trying to blackmail a star basketball player into throwing the big game. The detectives then spend the rest of the story trying to prevent the crime.

A Worthy Opponent

Regardless of when the reader discovers the villain's identity, your criminal should be as thought out and developed as the hero. Creating a memorable villain is key to success.

So what makes a villain memorable? Ironically some of the same qualities that make the hero unforgettable also make his or her opponent unforgettable: strength, cunning, determination. To ensure page-turning action in your story, your criminal must be capable of challenging your hero, physically and mentally. Until the end, he or she must stay one step ahead of your detective. The reader has to believe that the villain is capable of defeating the hero and getting away with his or her crimes.

Supporting Characters

What would Sherlock Holmes be without Dr. Watson? What would Nancy Drew do without help from her best friends, Bess and George? Dr. Watson, Bess, and George are supporting characters. As a general rule, supporting characters will not be suspects in your story (or will be eliminated as suspects early on). Instead, supporting characters serve many other purposes in mystery storytelling:

✔ They help complete tasks. Sometimes the help can be as simple as a boost up to a window or delivering a message for the hero. Sometimes supporters are needed to set traps.

✔ They act as sounding boards for the main characters. Sounding boards are especially useful in mysteries, as they allow the detective to speculate about clues out loud.

✔ They provide contrast. The down-to-earth Dr. Watson, for example, contrasts with the brainy, cold Sherlock Holmes. Contrast makes your characters stand out.

✔ They create obstacles and increase tension. Just like the story's villain, supporting characters can sometimes block or complicate the detective's path. Parent and teacher characters, for example, can use their authority to ground or delay the hero, thereby creating tension.

Creating 3-D Characters

Here are a few specific elements to consider when creating your unforgettable characters:

Looks. Looks can be deceiving . . . or not. Depending on how characters are being used in the story, their appearance may be either revealing or misleading. A man who is wearing a black, hooded sweatshirt and has a muscular frame, heavy eyebrows, and menacing eyes sounds dangerous and might make a great suspect. To keep your reader guessing, however, you might choose to make your villain's appearance misleading. The thieves in *Sammy Keyes and the Sisters of Mercy*, for example, dress up as nuns and seem harmless.

Occupations/Skills. Give your main characters jobs and skills that permit special access or power. For example, in *The Case of the Bizarre Bouquets,* the villain is a scam artist whose acting skills allow him to impress and to trick wealthy women. Detective Sammy Keyes is athletic. Being able to run fast and to kick and punch enables her to catch suspects and avoid injury. The journalist heroes of Feinstein's mysteries are not only good interrogators, but their press passes give them access to secret places and powerful people.

Character Development

Regardless of their roles in your mystery, your characters, especially your main ones, should be as developed and three-dimensional as possible. Once you have figured out the basic outline of your characters, start adding layers to their portraits. Think about the people you know. How many of them are all bad or all good? Always nice or always mean? Always smart or always slow? Real people have many sides and your characters should, too. Along with their dreams, they should have fears. They should have both strengths and weaknesses, virtues and faults.

Writing Exercise

Using an event or news story crime from the previous prompts, create biographies for your detective and criminal. Include the following elements:

Name (including nicknames) _____

Physical Traits:

Age _____   **Gender** _____

Body type (muscular, thin, petite, etc.) _____

Facial details (eye and hair color, nose, etc.)

_____

Clothing (sporty, formal, trendy, sloppy, etc.)

_____

Background:

Birthplace _____

Economic status (rich, poor, middle class) _____

Education (private school, public school, college degree, etc.)

_____

_____

Family life (siblings, parents, guardians, pets, etc.) _____

_____

_____

Where they are living now _____

Occupation (student, teacher, coach, etc.) _____

Personality traits (spunky, shy, intelligent, etc.) _____

_____

Dreams (list two) _____

_____

Fears (list two) _____

_____

Special skills (fast runner, photographic memory, etc.) _____

_____

Hobbies (drawing, photography, solving crossword puzzles, etc.)

_____

_____

Step 4

The Right Way to Write

You have finally figured out your plot, and you know your characters well. Your mystery is running through your head like a movie reel. You feel ready to write. But before putting pen to paper (or fingers to keyboard), you need to think about two key elements of storytelling: point of view and tense.

Point of View

Most mysteries are written from the point of view of a detective character. The detective describes the story's action and shares with the reader his or her thoughts about what has occurred. Sammy Keyes, Nancy Drew, and Enola Holmes are point-of-view detective characters.

In contrast, there are many other mysteries that are narrated from the perspective of a supporting character, or one member of a detective team. In the Sherlock Holmes mysteries, for example, Holmes's assistant, Dr. Watson, provides the mystery's point of view. In the Houdini and Nate mysteries, Nate is the point-of-view character, although Houdini performs half the action.

All these mysteries are written in limited third person. The action is seen through the eyes of the point-of-view character. In limited third-person narratives, the pronouns "he" or "she" stand in for the point-of-view character.

Some writers prefer to use the omniscient third person. "He" and "she" are used in omniscient third-person narrative, but the reader is not seeing the action through one particular character's eyes. Instead, the reader is experiencing the story from the writer's "all-seeing" perspective, like a camera looking down from above.

The following excerpt from Caroline Lawrence's Roman Mystery *The Pirates of Pompeii* is written in the omniscient third person. Although Lawrence gives the reader a sense of both character's emotions, neither character dominates the scene. Both girls, however, are detectives in the story:

> *The girls watched a coil of black smoke rise from the funeral pyre on the shore. Around it, tiny figures lifted their hands to the hot white sky and cried out to the gods. Nubia shuddered and reached for her mistress's hand.*
>
> *Flavia Gemina was more a friend than a mistress. A freeborn Roman girl, she had bought Nubia in the slave market of Ostia to save her from an unimaginable fate. Since then, Flavia's kindness had been like a drink of cool water in a desert of pain. Even now, Nubia took courage from Flavia's steady gaze and the reassuring squeeze of her hand.[1]*

Another narrative option is to write the story in the first person, using the pronoun "I" to stand in for the point-of-view character. As with limited third-person narration, first-person narration can describe only those physical details that the "I" person can see, hear, taste, smell, or feel. First-person narration tends to be more intense and personal than third person, but it can also be less flexible. R. L. Stine's *The Face* is written in first person.

Tense

Most mystery stories are written in the past tense. Even though the action may feel like it is happening in the present, the actual verb tense is past. It is important when writing any type of story to be consistent in your use of tense. Be careful to avoid slipping into the present tense as you are writing.

Active Action and Colorful Characters

Although mystery stories demand strong characters and solid plots, they also need powerful language to grab and hold the reader's attention. Consider this passage from *Nancy Drew: The Case of the Lost Song*:

> *"You won't believe this," Nancy started to say, when suddenly she heard a sound behind her. As she turned, she was blinded by a flash of light. Then she heard something whoosh through the air above her, and finally something crashed down on her head.*

Searing, hot pain exploded through Nancy's brain. Her knees buckled, and someone grabbed the phone from her hand. She heard the sound of the phone snapping closed, breaking the connection with George.

A moan escaped Nancy's lips as she dropped to the floor. She fought to stay conscious in order to focus on her assailant. But as the shadowy figure loomed above her, the room dissolved into blackness and she passed out.[2]

Words like flash, whoosh, crashed, and loomed take the reader right into the action. Active, colorful language can also help characters come alive. In *Danger in the Dark*, author Tom Lalicki describes Harry Houdini as follows:

Houdini was wearing opera clothes—a long, shiny black coat, a stiff white shirt, and a very pointy white bow tie. . . . His head was huge, or at least his head seemed huge on such a compact body. . . . His hair was thick and wiry like a scrub brush parted down the middle. Nathaniel noted how his eyes drew one in. All one could look at was Houdini's blue-gray eyes.[3]

In the above example, Lalicki follows a rule of thumb regarding physical descriptions—start with the largest element and work down to the smallest. Lalicki first gives the reader an impression of Houdini's whole body, including his unusual clothes. Then he describes Houdini's head, followed by the smaller details of his hair and eyes.

Using active, vibrant words makes your writing more enjoyable and easier to understand. If you become stumped for words, check a thesaurus or dictionary (available online or in your word-processing software) for suggestions.

One Room, Three Entrances

Compare these three sentences:

> The boy entered the room and sat down on the couch.

> The boy barreled into the room and threw himself on the couch.

> The boy stumbled into the room and collapsed on the couch.

The action described in all three sentences is the same: a boy goes into a room and sits on a couch. The second and third sentences, however, paint clearer and more intriguing pictures than the first. Both suggest something different. "Barreled" and "threw" suggest energy, while "stumbled" and "collapsed" imply exhaustion. By changing only a few words, you can increase and alter the impact of a sentence.

TMI

TMI (too much information) is another writing rule of thumb to remember. Describe only those aspects of a person or place that are striking or important to the plot. Too much information can bore and even confuse the reader. Lalicki, for example, describes Houdini's hair and eyes but says nothing about his nose, ears, or chin, focusing only on a few elements of Houdini's appearance that stand out the most.

Dialogue

No matter what type of mystery you are telling, you will probably want to include dialogue. Conversation among characters is one of the fastest and easiest ways to convey information to the reader. Whenever possible, try to give each of your characters a distinctive voice, or way of speaking, to showcase their personalities. Make your dialogue consistent and believable, keeping in mind each character's age, gender, and background.

Sometimes authors will suggest their characters' background by writing their dialogue with a regional accent. In the Enola Holmes mystery *The Case of the Bizarre Bouquets*, for example, author Nancy Parrish writes the Cockney English accent of one of her supporting characters this way:

> *"Miss Meshle," she declaimed with the bravado of one who decided to perform a Moral Duty, "it's no good yer shuttin' yerself up this way. Now whatever 'appened, and it's none of my business, but whatever it was, it's no use gittin' pale about.*[4]

In *Last Shot: A Final Four Mystery*, John Feinstein describes what the heavy Southern accent of his heroine, Susan Carol, sounds like to her Northern partner, Stevie:

> *"Oh, absolutely." (It came out abb-so-looo-taly.) "My daddy went to divinity school there and I've (aaahv) been a fan, I guess, since the cradle. I even got to talk to Coach K for my (mah) story. He was sooooo nice.*[5]

To get ideas for speaking styles, try recording friends and family and listen carefully for vocal quirks and accents. Do you hear certain phrases repeated over and over? Do they have noticeable accents? Do some speak loudly and others very softly? Are their voices pleasant or irritating?

Writing Exercises

Try the following activities, using characters and plot elements from previous steps.

1. Write the opening paragraph of your story. Then try rewriting the same paragraph from a different character's point of view.

2. Pick one character from your story and describe him or her from head to toe. Then rewrite the description, eliminating all but the most important physical details.

3. Pick two characters from your story and write a few lines of back-and-forth dialogue for them. Rewrite the dialogue using different accents or speaking styles and quirks. Does the new dialogue change the characters or the action in any way?

Step 5

Get Published!

So, you have completed your mystery. Your detective has solved the crime; the villain has been caught. Congratulations, the hard part is over! But your work is not quite done.

Rewriting

Before sending your story into the world, you need to do some fine-tuning and polishing. You need to rewrite. With mysteries in particular, you need to confirm that the story makes sense and that all the plot elements are in the right place.

Sometimes a plot point that seems obvious to the writer can be invisible to the reader. You may think you have included all the necessary information only to discover that your audience has been left in the dark. Or you may have revealed too much information too soon. To make sure that your mystery works, share your story with a few friends, teachers, or relatives. Were they able to follow your clues? Does your solution make sense? If your readers seemed confused, go back to your story charts or index cards to see if a different scene order might help or if you need to add new scenes or characters.

Formatting

If you have never written a story before, you may be unsure about proper formatting. Below is a short excerpt from *Last Shot: A Final Four Mystery* by John Feinstein, with added notes about formatting rules and techniques:

"So, what's our next move?" [*Place quotation marks around the first and last word in a line of dialogue.*] **Susan Carol asked as they walked into a surprisingly empty lobby.** [*Identify the speaker after dialogue when the speaker, in this case Susan Carol, is unknown to the reader.*]

Stevie tried to think. [*Begin a new paragraph each time you switch speakers.*] **"You still have those notes you made while I was writing?" he said.** [*There's no need to identify Stevie by name because he is mentioned earlier in the paragraph.*]

"Uh-huh, in my notebook." [*Start a new paragraph for new dialogue, but there's no need to identify the speaker.*]

"Okay. Let's sit down for a minute and go over what we know for sure. Then we can work on what we need to know and how to find out." [*A closing quotation mark goes after the last word of the dialogue, even though the dialogue continues for more than one sentence.*][1]

Here are a few more formatting rules to follow:

- **Start a new paragraph for descriptive, non-dialogue passages and also when the dialogue resumes.**

- **Always be clear about who is speaking. If the two characters who are speaking are different genders, you can use _he_ and _she_. Otherwise, be sure to use their names when switching between them.**

- **Add quotation marks around dialogue that is separated by a non-dialogue description, such as the phrase _she said_.**

Be Original

Although you are encouraged to read published mysteries for inspiration and guidance, you should always be original in your own writing. Deliberate copying of someone else's work is called plagiarism. When writing papers in English class, you can probably recall how much your teacher stressed the importance of paraphrasing and properly citing direct quotations. Avoiding plagiarism is just as important in creative writing as it is in academic writing. Copying includes using someone else's plot and characters as well as specific passages of text. Many publishers have computer programs that detect plagiarism, and plagiarism can lead to legal troubles.

Double-check Checklist

In addition to making sure the plot of your mystery works, check your writing for spelling, grammar, and style. Read each sentence slowly and carefully. Do your subject and verb match? Do your words actually mean what you think they mean? Are your verbs active? Are your adjectives and adverbs colorful? Does one sentence flow into the next? Is the tense consistent throughout?

Publish

Once you are satisfied that your mystery is as good as it can be and is original, you can submit it for publication. There are a number of online sites that accept stories from beginning writers. The Young Authors Guide section on Newpages.com offers a long list of publications that accept fiction by teen writers.

Web sites for reading and submitting teen fiction include MysteryNet.com, which specializes in mystery stories, Teen Ink, KidsBookshelf.com, Creative Kids Magazine, Inkpop, and Merlyn's Pen. Teen Ink also publishes a print magazine, available at libraries and through subscription.

You can also check out self-publishing companies, such as Lulu and Dog Ear Publishing. These companies allow you to print your own book, complete with cover and illustrations, for a small fee. Be aware that you will be required to sign a contract to publish through these companies.

Before submitting your work to specific publications, do some investigating. Find out what types of stories these publications prefer and who their target audiences are. Most youth-oriented magazines accept all types of writing, but some specialize in certain genres. To get a feel for the publication, read as many of its stories as you can, especially mysteries. You should also be sure that you meet the publication's age, language, gender, and geographic requirements. *Iguana* magazine, for example, only accepts stories written in Spanish, while *ChixLIT* only considers pieces written by girls. Some publications require that you live in a particular region or country.

Contests

Contests offer another way to get your story noticed and published. MysteryNet sponsors a contest for mystery stories written by kids for kids. The Amazing Kids! Web site sponsors an annual writing contest that honors different types of writing, including short stories and mysteries. Teen Ink awards fiction-writing prizes two times a year and publishes the winning stories in its print magazine. The Alliance for Young Artists & Writers also sponsors an annual writing contest for grades 7–12, which includes short-story and novel categories.

Other contests include the Young Voices Foundation short-story contest and Weekly Reader's online writing contest for teens.

Other Resources

If your school or community offers creative-writing courses or workshops, take them! Sharing your work with other aspiring writers can make rewriting easier and quicker. Reading your story out loud can help you pinpoint problem areas in your writing style and may even earn you applause!

If you live in the following cities, you may want to check out the local 826 organization, which offers free creative writing workshops and publishes student writing on a regular basis: Ann Arbor (826michigan), Boston (826 Boston), Chicago (826CHI), Los Angeles (826LA), New York (826NYC), San Francisco (826 Valencia), Seattle (826 Seattle), and Washington, D.C. (826DC).

Chapter Notes

Step 1: Finding Your Mystery Muse

1. Jacqueline Winspear, "Jacqueline Winspear's Backstory," *Backstory*, October 9, 2006, <http://mjroseblog.typepad.com/backstory/page/13/> (April 20, 2010).
2. Tom Knapp, "Nancy Springer: Writing What She Wants to Read," *Rambles*, 1989, <http://www.rambles.net/nancy_springer.html> (April 20, 2010).
3. R. L. Stine, *The Confession* (New York: Parachute Press, 1996), p. 3.
4. Knapp.

Step 4: The Right Way to Write

1. Caroline Lawrence, *The Pirates of Pompeii* (Brookfield, Conn.: Roaring Brook Press, 2003), p. 16.
2. Carolyn Keene, *Nancy Drew: The Case of the Lost Song* (New York: Pocket Books, 2001), p. 132.
3. Tom Lalicki, *Danger in the Dark: A Houdini and Nate Mystery* (New York: Farrar, Straus and Giroux, 2006), p. 54.
4. Nancy Springer, *The Case of the Bizarre Bouquets: An Enola Holmes Mystery* (New York: Philomel, 2008), p. 14.
5. John Feinstein, *Last Shot: A Final Four Mystery* (New York: Alfred A. Knopf, 2005), p. 14.

Step 5: Get Published!

1. John Feinstein, *Last Shot: A Final Four Mystery* (New York: Alfred A. Knopf, 2005), p. 74.

Glossary

alibi—An excuse that explains why a person could not have committed a crime based on his or her location.

clue—Any bit of information that helps in the solution of a mystery.

cozy mysteries—Mysteries in which the crime takes place before the story starts and that contain little or no violence.

deduction—A conclusion based on known facts or evidence.

dialogue—Conversation between two or more persons.

evidence—Gathered information that tends to prove or disprove something.

genre—A category of artistic work, such as a mystery.

hard-boiled detective mysteries—Mysteries that feature a tough private detective and contain violent action.

interrogate—To question, especially when seeking secret information.

investigation—An organized inquiry or quest to determine facts.

limited third person—Narration that is told from the point of view of a character represented by the pronouns "he" or "she."

motive—An inner urge that causes a person to act in a particular way.

muse—The source of artistic inspiration.

omniscient third person—"All-seeing" narration not told from any particular character's perspective.

plagiarism—Unauthorized use of another writer's thoughts and words.

plot—The arrangement of actions or happenings in a story.

police procedurals—Mysteries that focus on the details of police investigations, including scientific evidence and interrogations, usually featuring a police detective.

protagonist—The hero or main character of a story.

red herring—Information that misleads or stalls an investigation.

sleuth—A detective.

suspect—A person who is suspected of committing a crime.

suspense—A state of excitement, usually in anticipation of an unknown outcome.

victim—A person who is harmed by another's actions.

whodunit—A mystery that revolves around identifying a criminal from among a group of suspects.

witness—A person who saw a crime or has first-hand knowledge about a crime.

Further Reading

Books

Ellis, Sherry, and Laurie Lamson. *Now Write! Mysteries: Suspense, Crime, Thriller, and Other Mystery Fiction Exercises From Today's Best Writers and Teachers.* New York: Tarcher, 2011.

Emerson, Kathy Lynn. *How to Write Killer Historical Mysteries: The Art and Adventure of Sleuthing Through the Past.* McKinleyville, Calif.: Perseverance Press, 2008.

Hamilton, John. *You Write It: Mystery.* Edina, Minn.: ABDO and Daughters, 2009.

Landon, Lucinda. *Meg Mackintosh's Mystery Writing Handbook: For Young Authors and Illustrators.* Newport, R.I.: Secret Passage Press, 2012.

Internet Addresses

InfoSoup: Mysteries for Teens

http://info.infosoup.org/lists/TeenMysteries.asp

MysteryNet's Kids Mysteries

http://kids.mysterynet.com

Agatha Christie

http://www.agathachristie.com

Mildred Wirt Benson

http://www.nancydrewsleuth.com/mildredwirtbenson

PoeStories.com

http://www.poestories.com/

The World of R. L. Stine

http://www.rlstine.com

Sir Arthur Conan Doyle

http://www.sherlockholmesonline.org

Index